# Collins

# PRIMARY COMPREHENSION

## BOOK 1

### John Jackman

## Collins Educational

*An imprint of* HarperCollins*Publishers*

Published by Collins Educational
An imprint of HarperCollinsPublishers Ltd
77-85 Fulham Palace Road
London W6 8JB

© John Jackman 1997

First published 1997

Reprinted 1998 (twice)

ISBN 0 00 302304 4

John Jackman asserts the moral right to be identified as the author of this work.

Illustrations by Maggie Brand, Rob Englebright, Andrew Midgley, Rhiannon Powell, Martin Remphry.

British Library Cataloguing in Publication Data
A catalogue record for this book is available from the British Library.

Cover illustration: Martin Remphry
Editor: Claire Mayers
Designer: Neil Adams

Printed by Scotprint, Musselburgh

**Acknowledgements**
The author and publishers wish to thank the following for permission to use copyright material:
Faber and Faber Ltd for 'Roger the Dog' by Ted Hughes from *What is the Truth?*, 1984; David Higham Associates on behalf of the author for 'Big Bulgy Fat Black Slugs' by Berlie Doherty in Storychest, Kingscourt; Hodder & Stoughton Ltd for material from *Gumdrop Has a Birthday* by Val Biro, 1977; Frederick Warne & Co for illustrations and text from *The Tale of Peter Rabbit* by Beatrix Potter, © Frederick Warne & Co, 1902, 1987; The Watts Publishing Group for 'Isn't it Amazing' by Max Fatchen from *Peculiar Rhymes and Lunatic Lines*, Orchard Books, 1995.

Every effort has been made to trace the copyright holders, but if any have been inadvertently overlooked, the publishers will be pleased to make the necessary arrangement at the first opportunity.

# Contents

# Caterpillars

Wiggling, woggling up and down
Painted as bright as a circus clown
Clinging to twigs with tiny feet
Always looking for something to eat.
Some have bristles, some have spots
Some have patches like polka dots
They're brown and yellow, green and blue
But mostly green like the leaves they chew.

**Eric Slayter**

## Do you remember?

**Copy these sentences. Choose the correct word.**

1. The caterpillars look like _____ . (clowns **or** butterflies)
2. They are clinging to twigs with their _____ . (hands **or** feet)
3. They are looking for something to _____ . (eat **or** drink)
4. Caterpillars eat mostly _____ . (flowers **or** leaves)
5. _____ is the most usual colour of caterpillars. (Red **or** Green)

# More to think about

**Write a sentence to answer each question.**

1. In what way are some caterpillars like circus clowns?
2. Are all caterpillars smooth to touch?
3. What different sorts of patterns do caterpillars have on their bodies?
4. What is the most common colour of caterpillars?
5. Is it easier to spot a green or a red caterpillar on a green leaf?
6. Why is it better for caterpillars if they are not easy to find?

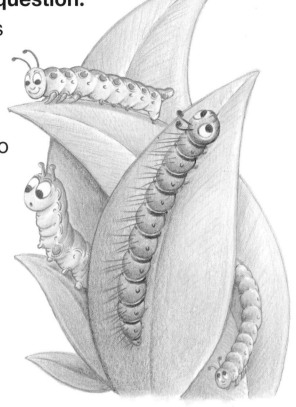

# Now try these

1. Find a word in the poem that rhymes with:
   a) down    b) feet    c) spots    d) blue

2. Match a word from each box to make pairs of words that have similar meanings, like this:

   **clinging = holding**

   | | |
   |---|---|
   | **clinging** | **chewing** |
   | **tiny** | **looking** |
   | **dots** | |

   | | |
   |---|---|
   | **searching** | **munching** |
   | **small** | **holding** |
   | **spots** | |

3. The poet says some caterpillars look like clowns. Make a list of anything else they remind you of.

# Working on a Farm

Look at these four pictures.
Farmer Lindsay is at work.

1 ploughing

2 raking the soil

3 sowing the seed

4 ?

# Do you remember?

**Copy these sentences. Choose the correct word.**

1. The _____ is Mr Lindsay.  (farmer **or** miner)
2. In picture 1 the farmer is _____ .  (sowing **or** ploughing)
3. After ploughing, he _____ the ground.  (rolls **or** rakes)
4. The ground is now ready for sowing the _____ .
   (buttons **or** seed)
5. The seed needs _____ to help it grow.  (rain **or** wind)

# More to think about

**Write sentences to answer these questions.**
**Some have been started to help you.**

1. Why does Farmer Lindsay need to plough the ground?
   The ground is ploughed so that ___pto_____ .
2. Why are the birds close by while the farmer is ploughing?
   The birds are _____ .
3. Does he sow the seed before or after raking?
   He sows _____ .
4. What sort of weather helps the seed to grow?
5. What job is being done in picture 4?
6. Which season does picture 4 show?

# Now try these

**Imagine you are a farmer. Make two lists in your book,**
**like this:**

| Things I **like** about being a farmer | Things I **dislike** about being a farmer |
| --- | --- |
|  |  |

# The Cow

The friendly cow all red and white,
　　I love with all my heart:
She gives me cream with all her might,
　　To eat with apple-tart.

She wanders lowing here and there,
　　And yet she cannot stray,
All in the pleasant open air,
　　The pleasant light of day:

And blown by all the winds that pass
　　And wet with all the showers,
She walks among the meadow grass
　　And eats the meadow flowers.

**Robert Louis Stevenson**

## Do you remember?

**Read these sentences about the poem.**
**Copy only the ones that are true.**

The cow is red and white.　　　　She lives all day in a barn.

She is not very friendly.　　　　When it rains she gets wet.

She likes to eat meadow flowers.　Her milk is made into cream.

She keeps getting out of her field.　The cow is black and white.

# More to think about

**Copy these sentences about the poem.**
**Choose the best ending for each one.**

1. The cow in the poem
   a) is friendly      b) is aggressive      c) is shy
2. Her coat is
   a) brown      b) red and white      c) black and white
3. Some of her milk is made into
   a) yoghurt      b) cheese      c) cream
4. She wanders about
   a) in silence      b) making contented sounds
   c) making a lot of noise
5. When it rains
   a) she gets wet      b) she is brought inside
   c) she keeps dry under the trees

# Now try these

1. Be a detective and think carefully about these questions.
   Write sentences in your book to answer each one.
   a) How do we know the poet probably owns the cow?
   b) Does he say he loves her with all his heart just because
      of the cream she gives? What other reasons might
      he have?
   c) What word does the poet use to make you know he likes
      the outdoor life?

2. Find these words in the poem. Write other words that mean
   the same.
   a) with all my heart      b) with all her might      c) pleasant

# The Three Billy Goats Gruff

The three Billy Goats Gruff had eaten all the leaves. They were getting very hungry.

Look, there are lots of fresh green leaves across the stream.

Let's cross the bridge and eat the leaves.

No! An ugly old troll is under the bridge. If we cross the bridge he will eat us up.

I am very hungry. I am going to cross the bridge. I'm not afraid of the ugly old troll.

Trip, trop, trip, trap, went Little Billy Goat Gruff.

Who is that on my bridge?

It's me! Little Billy Goat Gruff.

# Do you remember?

**Copy these sentences into your book.**
**Think of a sensible word to fill each gap.**

1. There were _____ billy goats.
2. They had eaten all the _____.
3. Now they were feeling very _____.
4. There were more leaves
   across the _____.
5. An ugly old _____
   lived under
   the bridge.

# More to think about

**Read these sentences about the story.**
**Write in your book 'true', 'false', or 'can't tell' for each one.**

1. There were three goats.
2. The goats were sisters.
3. They liked beech leaves more than ash leaves.
4. The troll was young.
5. Little Billy Goat Gruff was very hungry.
6. He said he wasn't afraid of the troll.

# Now try these

1. In your book write some sentences about the troll.
   Write about what he was like, and why you think he
   came to live under the bridge. Don't forget the
   capital letters and full stops.
2. Make up your own ending for this well-known story.
   Try to make it a surprise!

# Now isn't it amazing?

Now isn't it amazing
That seeds grow into flowers,
That grubs become bright butterflies
   And rainbows come from showers,
      That busy bees make honey gold
        And never spend time lazing,
          That eggs turn into singing birds,

     Now isn't that amazing?

**Max Fatchen**

## Do you remember?

**Copy these sentences.**
**Look at the poem and choose the correct word.**
1. Seeds grow into _____ . (flowers **or** butterflies)
2. Grubs turn into _____ . (birds **or** butterflies)
3. Rainbows come from sun and _____ . (wind **or** showers)
4. Bees make _____ . (jam **or** honey)
5. Birds grow from _____ . (worms **or** eggs)

## More to think about

**Look at the pictures. Match a sentence to each picture.**
**Write them in the correct order.**

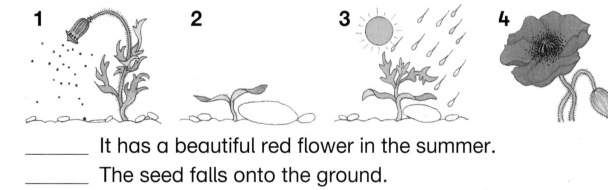

1        2        3        4

_____ It has a beautiful red flower in the summer.
_____ The seed falls onto the ground.
_____ The young plant begins to shoot.
_____ Rain keeps it damp and the sun keeps it warm.

## Now try these

1. Find a word in the poem that rhymes with:
   a) flowers    b) amazing
   Now think of other words that rhyme with each of
   these words.
2. What is the most amazing thing you have ever seen or
   heard about? Say why you think it is so special.

# Looking at Books

## Do you remember?

**Copy these sentences. Choose words from
the box to fill the gaps.**

> Keeping Small Animals    James Matthews
>
> writes    Sarah Richards    draws

1. The title of the book is _____ .
2. The author of the book is called _____ .
3. An author is the person who _____ the words.
4. The name of the illustrator of the book is _____ .
5. An illustrator is the person who _____ the pictures.

## More to think about

**Look at these book covers. Write numbers to answer each question.**

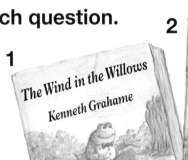

1. Which is the story book?
2. In which book could I check the meaning of a word?
3. Which book did Hilary Frost write?
4. In which book might I find facts about rabbits?
5. Which book will help me check the spelling of a word?
6. Which book might tell me about the River Amazon?
7. Which of the books was written by Kenneth Grahame?
8. In which **two** books might I discover more about where alligators live?

## Now try these

**Write the title and author of one of each of these types of book that you can find in your classroom.**

A book that:

1. tells you about birds
2. has a story
3. helps you with spelling words
4. has lots of pictures
5. is about another country
6. is your favourite

Some of the books you choose might have more than one author.

# Gumdrop has a Birthday

Mr Oldcastle has invited several of his friends to help celebrate Gumdrop's birthday. After they have given Gumdrop his presents ...

... the guests gathered round Gumdrop to wish him
Many Happy Returns and another fifty years of happy motoring.
"For he's a jolly good fellow," they sang, and
"Happy birthday, dear Gumdrop, happy birthday to you!"

Mr Oldcastle was very happy and he thanked them all
for Gumdrop's sake.
"And here is the birthday cake!" he said.
But it wasn't on the table – and it hadn't rolled away.
It had vanished!
"Who took the cake?" he cried.

Horace was very happy too.
He sat on the ground and he looked very fat.
There wasn't a crumb to be seen,
because he likes cakes.

**Val Biro**

## Do you remember?

**Write the correct answer to each question in your book.**
1. Whose birthday is it?
   a) It is Gumdrop's birthday.    b) It is Mr Oldcastle's birthday.
2. What is Gumdrop?
   a) Gumdrop is a van.      b) Gumdrop is an old car.

3. Was the birthday cake on the table?

    a)  No, the cake had vanished.

    b)  Yes, the cake was on the table.

4. What is the name of Mr Oldcastle's dog?

    a)  The dog's name is Rover.   b)  The dog's name is Horace.

## More to think about

Here are the instructions for making Gumdrop's birthday cake. They are in the wrong order. Write them out correctly in your book.

Put the ingredients in a bowl.

Stir the ingredients.

Bake the mixture in the oven.

Wash your hands.

Ice the cake and put on the candles.

Go to the shop to buy the ingredients.

## Now try these

1. Read these sentences about the story. Write in your book 'true', 'false', 'probably' or 'can't tell' for each one.

    a)  Mr Oldcastle is very fond of Gumdrop.

    b)  Gumdrop is 50 years old.

    c)  Mr Oldcastle is the most popular person in the village.

    d)  The birthday cake vanished.

    e)  The cake had rolled under Gumdrop.

    f)  Horace had eaten the cake.

2. Imagine you are Horace. Tell the story of the birthday party from your point of view.

# UNIT 8

# An Ants' Nest

Have you sat on a path on a warm summer's day, watching a line of ants marching busily to and fro? They are probably worker ants going to their nearby nest. Here is a page from a book about ants.

## Inside the nest
Tiny tunnels lead into the nest.
Each nest is a mass of tunnels and rooms.

## Types of ant
In every nest there are three types of ant.
The biggest are the queen ants. Queen ants have wings.
The big males also have wings, but aren't quite as big.
The small ants are the worker ants, and they don't have wings.

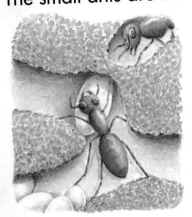

## Who does what?
A queen ant lives in one room of the nest. She stays in her room all the time and lays hundreds of eggs.
The big male mates with a queen, then dies. The worker ants collect the food. They feed the young ants, keep the nest clean, and dig more rooms and tunnels as they are needed. They also keep away ants from other nests.

## Do you remember?

**Copy these sentences. Fill in the missing words.**

1. Inside an ants' nest is a mass of t_____ and rooms.
2. There are t_____ types of ant.

3. The biggest ants are the q_____ .
4. W_____ ants are the smallest.
5. A queen ant's main job is to lay the e_____ .

## More to think about

1. Write a sentence to answer each question.
    a) What are the three types of ant?
    b) Which two types of ant have wings?
    c) Who looks after the young ants?
    d) Why do there need to be so many worker ants for each queen?
    e) Which ants have the shortest life?
2. Write a sentence to answer each question.
    a) Write one fact about male ants.
    b) Write two facts about queen ants.
    c) Write three facts about worker ants.

## Now try these

1. Imagine you suddenly shrink, and became ant-sized. You explore an ants' nest.
   Make two lists to show in what ways ants are similar to humans, and the things that are different. Like this:

| Ways ants are similar to humans | Ways ants are different from humans |
| --- | --- |
|  |  |

2. Ants are tiny, but when they work together they can do things they couldn't manage by themselves. Write down five things you can do alone, and five things you can do only with other people to help.

# Thunder and Lightning

This is an old African legend.

Thunder and Lightning were two grumpy old sheep. Lightning would lose his temper and knock down trees and burn the crops. Thunder, his mother who had an extremely loud voice, would shout at him.

The villagers became really fed up with them.
The villagers kept complaining about the damage – and the noise!
In the end, the village chief said he couldn't stand it any longer. He said they would have to go far away. He sent them to live in the sky!

But things didn't work out as the chief intended. To this day, Lightning still enjoys getting his own back on the villagers, and Thunder still shouts at the top of her voice and keeps the villagers awake at night.

## Do you remember?

**Write the correct answer to each question in your book.**

1. Did this legend come from Africa?
   a) No, this legend came from America.
   b) Yes, this legend came from Africa.
2. What were Thunder and Lightning?
   a) Thunder and Lightning were sheep.
   b) Thunder and Lightning were old men.

3. What did Lightning do to the crops?
   a) Lightning burnt the crops.
   b) Lightning watered the crops.
4. Where did the village chief send them?
   a) The village chief sent them to live in
      the sky.
   b) The village chief sent them to the shops.

## More to think about

**Write these sentences neatly in your book in
the correct order to make a story.**
1. Lightning still upsets the villagers.
2. He sent them away to live in the sky.
3. Thunder and Lightning were two troublesome sheep.
4. The villagers became very annoyed.
5. Thunder still grumbles away in her loud, booming voice.
6. Eventually the village chief could stand it no longer.

## Now try these

1. Copy these two lists of words into your book. Draw lines
   to join words that have similar meanings. One has been
   done to help you.

   | | |
   |---|---|
   | fed up | naughty |
   | complain | in the end |
   | banished | sent away |
   | eventually | object to |
   | troublesome | annoyed |

2. Imagine that you were a villager in this legend. Write in
   your book about what happened, what you did about it,
   and how you felt.

# The Lion and the Mouse

One day a mouse happened to run over the paws of a sleeping lion. Angrily the mighty beast woke. He was about to crush the little animal when the mouse cried out, "Please, mighty king of all the animals, spare me. I would be only a tiny mouthful, and I'm sure you would not like the taste. Besides, I might be able to help you some day. You never can tell."

The idea that this tiny creature could ever help him amused the lion so much that he let his little prisoner go.

Some time after this the lion, roaming in the forest for food, was caught in a hunter's net. The more he struggled the more he became stuck; his roar of rage echoed through the forest. Hearing the sound the mouse ran to the trap and began to gnaw the ropes that bound the lion. It was not long before he had bitten through the last cord with his little teeth and set the huge beast free.

**Don't belittle little things.**

**Aesop's Fables**

## Do you remember?

**Write 'true', 'false' or 'can't tell' for each of these sentences.**

1. The mouse pulled the lion's tail to wake him.
2. The lion was angry.

3. He ate the little mouse.
4. When the lion was trapped the mouse released him.
5. The animals lived in Africa.

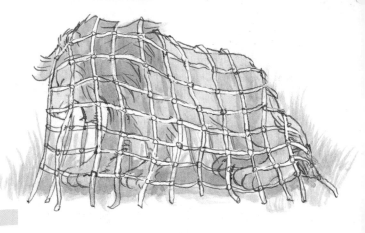

## More to think about

1. Write a sentence to answer each of these questions.
   a) What was the lion going to do when the mouse woke him?
   b) What made the lion change his mind?
   c) Who was 'the little prisoner'?
   d) How did the mouse know the lion was in trouble?
   e) How did the mouse rescue the lion?

2. These sentences have been muddled up.
   Write them in the correct order.
   a) The mouse persuaded the lion to set him free.
   b) The lion was trapped in the forest.
   c) A little mouse woke a lion.
   d) The lion grabbed the mouse.
   e) The mouse helped the lion to escape.
   f) The lion was going to eat the mouse.

## Now try these

1. Have you ever been frightened by someone bigger than you? Write some sentences about what happened and how you felt.
2. Aesop's fables often have a moral. The moral of this story is:
   **Don't belittle little things.**
   Write what you think it means.

# Crash!

1. window  watching
2. aeroplane  crash
3. parachute  pilot
4. telephone  help
5. rescued  helicopter
6. reward

# Do you remember?

**Copy these sentences into your book.**
**Think of a sensible word to fill each gap.**

1. The girls were looking out of their _____ .
2. They saw a plane _____ into the sea.
3. The pilot came down with his _____ .
4. The girls called for _____ .
5. A _____ went to rescue the pilot.
6. The pilot gave the girls a _____ for saving his life.

# More to think about

1. Write an interesting sentence about each of the six pictures on the left.
2. Planes and helicopters travel in the air.
   Sort the words below into their correct lists.

| helicopter ship van bike ferry coach plane |
| glider aircraft carrier canoe car hot air balloon |

| Travel in the air | Travel on land | Travel on water |
| --- | --- | --- |

# Now try these

**In your book write ...**

1. what the telephone operator said when the girls called ...
2. what the pilot said when the helicopter arrived ...
3. what their teacher said when the girls told her the story!

# UNIT 11 The Dragon's Cold

Do you enjoy a visit to a beach? When these friends visited a beach they were in for a surprise that they weren't expecting.

"Look at this," said Mimi. "Look what I've found!"

"It's very long," said Alex.

"And it's incredibly heavy," said Roland.

"What can it be?" asked Spike.

"It's a dragon!" they all shouted.

"Let's get out of here!"

"Oh, don't go," said the dragon.

"I won't hurt you." He sounded very sad.

"What's the matter?" asked Mimi.

"It's this dreadful cold," sniffed the dragon.

"It's completely put my fire out. All my family and friends sent me away. 'Duncan,' they said, 'no one wants a dragon without fire.'"

"We want you," said Mimi, "and we'll take care of you."

"We'll think of something," agreed Alex.

**John Talbot**

# Do you remember?

**Copy these sentences. Choose the correct ending.**

1. Mimi found a _____ . (dragon **or** octopus)
2. The dragon was very _____ . (short **or** long)
3. His name was _____ . (Duncan **or** Dingwall)
4. He seemed rather _____ . (happy **or** sad)
5. Duncan had lost his _____ . (fire **or** hat)

# More to think about

**Write a sentence to answer each question.**

1. How many friends were on the beach?
2. Do you think they went to the beach to look for dragons?
3. Why were they going to run away?
4. Why had Duncan lost his fire?
5. What do you think happened in the end?

# Now try these

1. Make two lists in your book.
   List 1: The best things about being a dragon.
   List 2: The worst things about being a dragon.
2. Write about how you would have felt if you were Duncan and your family sent you away.

# Fun on Bikes

## ANNUAL YOUNG BIKERS' CHAMPIONSHIP

Crossfield Farm, Westergate
Saturday 25th October

Juniors (7-10 years) 10.00 – 12.30
Seniors (11-14 years) 12.30 – 3.00

(Sorry – No under-7 bikers
allowed to enter)

Entrance fees:
Riders free  Spectators £1.00

Refreshment Tent

## Do you remember?

**Copy these sentences.
Choose the best ending.**

1. There is going to be a — bike-riding championship.
   — road safety competition.

2. It will be held on — Friday 24th October.
   — Saturday 25th October.

3. Junior events are — in the morning.
   — in the afternoon.

4. Riders under 7 — are allowed to ride.
   — are not allowed to ride.

5. The entrance fee for adults — is £1.
   — is free.

## More to think about

**Write a sentence to answer each question.**

1. Where are the championships to be held?
2. How much does it cost to enter?
3. If you are 9, what time are your races?
4. Your sister is 13. What time are her competitions?
5. Can you buy food and drinks after the races?

## Now try these

1. Copy these lists of words. Draw a neat line to join the words that have similar meanings.

    annual                  competition
    championship            charge
    fee                     once a year
    spectators              things to eat and drink
    refreshments            audience

2. Think carefully, then write in your book how you would feel if each of these things happened:
    a) You are given a new mountain bike as a present.
    b) The car taking you to the championships breaks down on the way.
    c) You win your first ever race.
    d) You reach the final, but then come last!
    e) Your little sister wins the cup in her event.

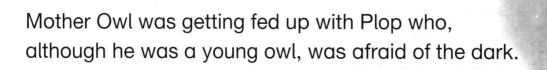

# The Owl Who Was Afraid of the Dark

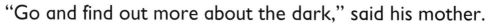

Mother Owl was getting fed up with Plop who,
although he was a young owl, was afraid of the dark.

"Go and find out more about the dark," said his mother.
"Ask that little girl down there what she thinks about it."
"What little girl?"
"That little girl sitting down there – the one with the pony-tail."
"Little girls don't have **tails**."
"This one does. Go on now or you'll miss her."
So Plop shut his eyes, took a deep breath, and fell off his branch.
His landing was a little better than usual. He bounced three times
and rolled gently towards the little girl's feet.
"Oh, a woolly ball!" cried the little girl.
"Actually, I'm a Barn Owl," said the woolly ball.
"An owl? Are you sure?" she said, putting out a grubby finger and
prodding Plop's round fluffy tummy.
"Quite sure," said Plop, backing away and drawing himself up tall.
"Well, there's no need to be huffy," said the little girl. "You bounced.
You must expect to be mistaken for a ball if you go bouncing about
the place. I've never met an owl before. Do you say 'Tu-wit-a-woo'?"
"No," said Plop, "that's Tawny Owls."
"Oh, you can't be a proper owl then," said the little girl. "**Proper**
owls say 'Tu-wit-a-woo'!"
"I **am** a proper owl!" said Plop, getting very cross. "I am a Barn
Owl, and Barn Owls go "**Eeeek**" like that. Anyway – you can't be a
proper girl. Girls don't have **tails**. Squirrels have tails, rabbits have
tails, mice ..."

**Jill Tomlinson**

30

## Do you remember?

**Match these questions and answers. Write them in your book. The first one has been done for you.**

1. Where was the little girl? **The little girl was below the tree.**
2. Why did Plop think the girl had a tail?
3. Could Plop fly well?
4. What sort of owl was Plop?

> No, Plop couldn't fly very well.
> Plop was a Barn Owl.
> The girl's hair was in a pony-tail.
> The little girl was below the tree.

## More to think about

1. Which words in the story tell us that:
   a) Plop was worried about flying
   b) he didn't yet have his adult feathers
   c) the little girl had dirty hands?
2. Write three sentences in your book about Plop. Think about his personality as well as what he looked like. Don't forget to use capital letters and full stops.

## Now try these

1. The little girl said Plop was like a 'woolly ball'. Write in your book some words to describe these birds and animals:
   a) giraffe   b) hippopotamus   c) robin   d) kitten
2. Have you ever been frightened of the dark, like Plop? Make a list of the things about the dark that can sometimes frighten people.

# UNIT 14 Lost in the Zoo

Dinesh and Indira have been taken to the zoo by their grandparents.

They were having such a good time feeding the lambs that they didn't notice that they had become lost in the crowds. Luckily Indira had a map of the zoo.

## Do you remember?

**Copy these sentences. Fill in the missing words.**

1. The children's names are _____ and _____ .
2. Their _____ had taken them to the zoo.
3. They were feeding the _____ .
4. They didn't notice they were _____ .
5. Luckily Indira had a _____ .

## More to think about

**Write a sentence to answer each question.**

1. Where were Dinesh and Indira feeding the lambs?
2. What was their quickest way back to the ticket office?
3. Which animals are kept closest to the ticket office?
4. What type of sea animal would they have seen as they walked back to the office?
5. Grandad left a message at the office to meet at the exit. Describe the best route from the office to the exit.
6. Which creatures did they see sharing an enclosure with the pelicans?
7. What animals were sharing with the zebras?
8. If they had gone to the exit straight from Pets' Corner, which two roads would they have walked along?

## Now try these

Can you remember ever being lost? Imagine you are Dinesh or Indira and you are lost in this crowded zoo on a very hot day. Write some sentences about how you are feeling and what you are thinking.

Peter lived with his family in a sand-bank, under the roots of a big fir tree. He was always a problem for his mother, causing trouble and getting into scrapes.

"Now, my dears," said old Mrs Rabbit one morning, "you may go into the fields or down the lane, but don't go into Mr McGregor's garden. Your father had an accident there; he was put into a pie by Mrs McGregor. Now run along and don't get into mischief. I am going out."

Flopsy, Mopsy and Cotton-tail went down the lane to gather blackberries. But Peter, who was very naughty, ran straight away to Mr McGregor's garden and squeezed under the gate!

First he ate some lettuces and some French beans; and then he ate some radishes; and then, feeling rather sick, he went to look for some parsley. But round the end of the cucumber frame, who should he meet but Mr McGregor!

Mr McGregor was on his hands and knees planting out young cabbages, but he jumped up and ran after Peter, waving a rake and calling out, 'Stop thief!'

Peter rushed all over the garden, for he had forgotten the way back to the gate. He lost one of his shoes among the cabbages, and then the other shoe among the potatoes. After losing them, he ran on four legs and went faster, so I think he might have got away altogether if he had not unfortunately run into a gooseberry net and got caught by the large buttons on his jacket.

Adapted from **Beatrix Potter**

## Do you remember?

**Finish these sentences. Write them in your book.**

1. Mrs Rabbit told her children they must not _____.
2. Flopsy, Mopsy and Cotton-tail went to gather _____.
3. Peter got into Mr McGregor's garden by _____.
4. When Mr McGregor saw Peter he _____.

## More to think about

**Match these questions and answers. Write them in your book. The first one has been done for you.**

1. What had happened to Mr Rabbit?

   **Mr Rabbit had been put into a pie.**
2. What did Peter eat in the garden?
3. What was Mr McGregor doing in the garden?
4. Was Peter frightened when he saw Mr McGregor?
5. What did Peter lose among the cabbages?

> Peter was very frightened when he saw Mr McGregor.
> Mr McGregor was planting out young cabbages.
> Peter lost a shoe among the cabbages.
> Peter ate some lettuces, French beans and radishes.

## Now try these

1. Copy these words from the story. Then next to each, write another word the writer could have used, like this:

   a) mischief  trouble        b) among
   c) gather                   d) rushed
2. In your book write what Mr McGregor might have said to his wife when he went in for his tea.

# Roger the Dog

Asleep he wheezes at his ease.
He only wakes to scratch his fleas.

He hogs the fire, he bakes his head
As if he were a loaf of bread.

He's just a sack of snoring dog.
You lug him like a log.

You can roll him with your foot,
He'll stay snoring where he's put.

I take him out for exercise,
He rolls in cowclap up to his eyes.

He will not race, he will not romp,
He saves his strength for gobble and chomp.

He'll work as hard as you could wish
Emptying his dinner dish,

Then flops flat, and digs down deep,
Like a miner, into sleep.

**Ted Hughes**

## Do you remember?

**Copy these sentences. Choose the correct word.**

1. Roger only wakes to scratch his _____ . (tummy **or** fleas)
2. He likes sleeping by the _____ . (fire **or** radiator)
3. Roger _____ a lot. (barks **or** snores)
4. He likes eating and _____ best. (sleeping **or** running)
5. The only hard work he does is _____ . (eating **or** digging)

## More to think about

1. The poet chooses words to make an interesting
   word picture. Copy these lists and draw lines to words
   with similar meanings. One has been done for you.

| Poet's words | similar words |
|---|---|
| wheezes | run and jump about |
| bakes | breathes noisily |
| lug him | eat |
| romp | lies down |
| gobble and chomp | carry him |
| flops flat | warms |

2. Find a word in the poem that rhymes with:
   a) head   b) log   c) put   d) eyes
   e) romp   f) dish   g) fleas   h) deep

## Now try these

1. Imagine Roger is your dog. Describe what happened
   when you wanted to take him to the shops with you.
   Think about what passers by might have been saying!

2. If you could choose any animal as a pet, what would
   you choose? Write three reasons for your choice.

3. Write a nonsense verse. Try to think of four other animals.

If I met a crocodile
   I'd run a mile
If I met a _____
   I'd _____

# UNIT 17

# Gran's New House

'Seaview'
Cliff Lane,
Sandy Bay,
SY13 7AB

Saturday 6th May.

Dear Annie, Tim and Jenny,

We moved into our new house just three days ago. I think we are going to like it, even though it is strange not living in the same town as you any more. From our front windows we can see the sea, and at the back we have lovely views of the hills.

The removal truck broke down so it took us six hours to get here, when it should have only taken about two hours!

Grandad and I thought you might like to come and stay for a few days in the school holidays. If Mum and Dad can't come, then we'll meet you at the station.

With much love,

Gran xxx

## Do you remember?

**Copy these sentences. Fill in the missing words.**

1. Gran and Grandad have moved to _____.
2. They moved _____ days ago.
3. From the front windows they can see the _____.
4. The removal truck took _____ hours to get to Sandy Bay.

## More to think about

1. Write a sentence to answer each question.

   a) On which day of the week did Gran and Grandad move into their new house?
   b) What will they miss most living in Sandy Bay?
   c) What is Jenny's brother's name?
   d) When can the children go to visit their grandparents?
   e) How might the children get to Sandy Bay if their parents are at work?

2. Spot the mistakes. Write the sentences correctly in your book.

   a) Gran enjoys watching the ships from the back window of her house.
   b) The hills are in front of their new house.
   c) It took six hours to mend the removal truck.
   d) Gran says the children can't come and stay.
   e) Gran and Grandad will meet the children at the bus stop.

## Now try these

Describe how you imagine Gran and Grandad's new house. Write a few sentences about what it looks like and where it is.

# Hot Dog Harris

The Harris family had a dog. Nothing unusual about that you might think – except Hot Dog Harris was the smallest dog in the world!

Hot Dog was a Yorkshire terrier. He lived in Barnsley with Mr and Mrs Harris and their son Harold and their daughter Hattie and their grandad, old Mr Harris.

Old Mr Harris didn't think much of Hot Dog. "You call that a dog!" he said. "It looks like a wig on legs."

Hot Dog was so small everyone had to be very careful around him.

Old Mr Harris had to be very careful where he sat down.
Mrs Harris had to be careful when she hoovered the carpet.
Mr Harris had to be careful whenever he blew his nose.
Harold had to be careful whenever he put on his football boots.
Hattie had to be careful to look before she jumped into bed.
They all had to be careful not to let Hot Dog out of the house.

He was so small anything might happen!

**Rose Impey**

## Do you remember?

**Copy these sentences into your book.**
**Think of a sensible word to fill each gap.**

1. Hot Dog was a Yorkshire _____.
2. He lived with the _____ family.

3. They all lived in a town called _____ .
4. The children were called _____ and _____ .
5. Grandad said Hot Dog looked like a _____ on legs.

## More to think about

1. One word in each sentence doesn't make sense.
   Write each sentence correctly in your book.
   a) Harold's brother was called Hattie.
   b) Hot Dog was the longest dog in the world.
   c) Their grandad loved the little creature.
2. Write a sentence to answer each question.
   a) Why do you think the dog was called 'Hot Dog'?
   b) Why did old Mr Harris call him 'a wig on legs'?
   c) Why did the family want to keep Hot Dog in the house?

## Now try these

1. Pretend you are Hot Dog. Copy these boxes neatly into
   your book. Write two ideas in each box. One has been
   done to help you.

| Good things about being small | Good things about being big |
|---|---|
| My owners can take me about easily. | |
| Bad things about being small | Bad things about being big |
| | |

2. One day Hot Dog managed to escape from the house.
   Describe one of the adventures he might have had.

# Funny Feeders

Many **toads** have long tongues. They can shoot them out extremely quickly to catch their food, usually an insect. Then they bring their tongue – and the insect – back into their mouth.

**Vultures** don't kill animals. They circle around waiting for an animal to die, or be killed. Then they swoop down to feed.

Many insects eat plants, but **Venus fly traps** are plants that attack insects! They trap the insect in their leaves, which close together until the insect dies.

Some plants live off other plants. They feed off the other plant without killing it. We call these parasites. **Mistletoe**, which grows in the branches of trees, is one of these.

**Mosquitoes** and some other small creatures, like **fleas**, are also parasites. They live on other animals (including people sometimes!) by making tiny holes through the skin and sucking blood.

## Do you remember?

**Copy these sentences into your book.**
**Think of a sensible word to fill each gap.**

1. Some toads have long _____ .
2. Vultures wait for animals to _____ .
3. Venus fly traps catch _____ in their leaves.
4. Mistletoe grows in _____ .
5. Mosquitoes and fleas are both called _____ .

## More to think about

**Write a sentence to answer**
**each question.**

1. Why are vultures good for
   the environment?
2. Why would it be bad for the parasite
   if it killed the plant or animal it lives on?
3. Why is mistletoe becoming a rare plant in many places?
4. If you squash a mosquito it leaves a red mark. Why?

## Now try these

Imagine you are a creature that has just arrived from outer
space. You have never seen humans before. Write a report
about how these strange human creatures feed. Start like this,
or make up your own beginning if you prefer:

First they dig up funny lumpy things from the ground,
which they put into boiling water. They also put other
plants in hot water and watch them go all squidgy
and squashy.

# Big bulgy fat black slugs

Berlie Doherty wrote this poem when her young daughter ran into the garden in bare feet – and got a slug stuck between her toes!

I don't like
big bulgy black fat slugs.
I don't know why.

When they creep along,
soft and slimy and squashy,
wobbly and wet,
in the long grass;

and when they slide,
their slippery trail
squelchy blobs
along the path;

and when they curl up,
cold and slithery
if I touch one by mistake;

and when they squidge
between my toes
if I'm running
in bare feet ...

that's when I know,
I know for sure,
I wouldn't want one
for a pet.

## Do you remember?

**Copy these sentences.**
**Choose a word from the box to fill in the missing words.**

| pet | slugs | toes | grass | path |

1. The poet doesn't like _____ .
2. She says they are wobbly and wet in the long _____ .

3. They leave their slippery trails along the _____ .

4. She doesn't want them to get between her _____ .

5. She definitely wouldn't want a slug as a _____ .

## More to think about

**Look at the poem again. One word in each sentence doesn't make sense. Write each sentence correctly in your book.**

1. Slugs are usually yellow.
2. They jump through wet grass.
3. When they swim they leave a slippery trail.
4. Slugs explode between your toes.

## Now try these

1. Write the words the poet uses to describe these. The first one has been done to help you.

   a) what slugs look like   **big bulgy black**

   b) how slugs look when they creep

   c) how slugs look when they slide

   d) how slugs feel if you touch them

2. Make a list of your four favourite creatures. Say why you like each one.

3. Make a list of four creatures you don't like. Say what it is you don't like about each one.

4. Imagine the slug could understand English, and heard people saying unkind and rude things about him. How would he feel, and what might he say back?

# The Golly Sisters Go West

The Golly Sisters sat in their wagon.
They were going west.
"Go," May-May said to the horse.
The horse did not go.

"This makes me mad," May-May said.
"Our wagon is ready. Our songs and
dances are ready. And the horse
will not go."

"It makes me mad too," said Rose.
"Something is wrong with this horse."

Rose got down from the wagon. May-May got down too.
They walked around the horse.

"Do you see anything wrong?" May-May asked.
"No, but something is wrong," said Rose.
"When we say, 'Go,' the horse does not go."
"And if the horse does not go, we do not go," said May-May.

Suddenly, Rose said, "Sister! I just remembered something.
There is a horse word for 'go'."
"A horse word?" said May-May.
"What is it?"
"Giddy-up!" Rose said.

The horse went.

**Betsy Byers**

## Do you remember?

**What words are missing from the passage? Write them in.**

____1____ and ___2___, the two Golly sisters, couldn't make their ___3___ go. The ___4___ was loaded, and they had practised their ___5___ and ___6___. The sisters got very ___7___, but the horse still wouldn't go! Then Rose remembered you need to say ___8___ to tell a horse to go.

## More to think about

1. Write a sentence to answer each question.
   a) Where were the Golly sisters going?
   b) How do you know they didn't drive wagons very often?
   c) Was the horse well trained or badly trained?
   d) Were they right to get cross with the horse?
   e) Did getting cross with the horse make it go?
2. Write a short version of the story so far, using no more than three sentences.
3. How do you think the story of the Golly sisters might have ended?

## Now try these

Think of a time when something didn't happen that you have really wanted to happen, like:
> when you couldn't make a new computer game work,

**or** when you couldn't get the chain back on your bike,

**or** when someone you had been expecting didn't turn up.
Write some sentences about what you did and how you felt.